DATE DUE

Tall If

New Issues Poetry & Prose

A Green Rose Book

New Issues Poetry & Prose
The College of Arts and Sciences
Western Michigan University
Kalamazoo, Michigan 49008

First Edition, 2008.

ISBN-10   1-930974-78-7 (paperbound)
ISBN-13   978-1-930974-78-4 (paperbound)

Library of Congress Cataloging-in-Publication Data:
Irwin, Mark
Tall If/Mark Irwin
Library of Congress Control Number: 2008923667

Editor	William Olsen
Managing Editor	Marianne Swierenga
Copy Editor	Natalie Giarratano
Designer	Danielle Webb
Art Director	Tricia Hennessy
Production Manager	Paul Sizer
	The Design Center, Frostic School of Art
	College of Fine Arts
	Western Michigan University
Printing	Cushing-Malloy, Inc.

Tall If

Mark Irwin

New Issues

WESTERN MICHIGAN UNIVERSITY

Also by Mark Irwin

Collections of Poetry:

The Halo of Desire
Against the Meanwhile
Quick, Now, Always
White City
Bright Hunger

Limited Editions:

Umbrellas in the Snow
Rodeo
Long Portrait

Translations:

Notebook of Shadows: Selected Poems of Philippe Denis
    (1974-1980)
Ask the Circle to Forgive You: Selected Poems of Nichita Stanescu
    (1964-1979); (With Mariana Carpinisan)

for Lisa Utrata,

& in memory of Randi Schulman (1949-2007),
Jim Simmerman (1952-2006)
& Carroll Cassill (1929-2008)

Contents

Doors   7

I.

Theory   11
Voice, Distant, Still Assembling   12
The Irises   13
Poem   14
Paradise   15
The Nest   17
Elegy (With Advertisement) Struggling to Find
    its Hero   18
When I Died   20
Psalm   21
Joy   22
Little Opus, Leaning, At That   23
Landscape with Ball, Then Smeared with Shadow   24
Call   25

II.

Tall If   29
American Urn   30
Aria (With a Hole in It)   31
Sunday   32
Weight of Light   33
Yes   34
Concrete   35
Now   36
Heart   37
The Field   38
Epic Detour   39
Résumé   40

III.

Gone   45
Passage   46
Landscape Crossed with Sleep & Prayer   47
The Mountain   48
Home   50
A Brief History of Eternity   51
Icon   52
Stadium   53
Hello   54

IV.

Blueprint for Civilization Sometimes Lost in
    Frivolous Detail   59
Church Engine   60
What I Remember   61
Liminal, Bridal, Tremulous   62
Ars Poetica   63
Soul?   64
Long Portrait   65
The Lastingness of Things Only Occurs in
    a Brief Light   66
Searchlight   67
Eurydice & Orpheus   68
Politics   69
Panels   70
Ends   71
After   72

"He whom you cannot teach to fly, teach him to fall faster."
—Nietzsche, *Thus Spoke Zarathustra*

I've known a Heaven, like a Tent—
To wrap its shining Yards—
Pluck up its stakes, and disappear—
Without the sound of Boards
Or Rip of Nail—Or Carpenter—
But just the miles of Stare—
—Emily Dickinson, #243

"There is no steady unretracing progress in this life: we
do not advance through fixed gradations, and at the last one pause: —
through infancy's unconscious spell, boyhood's thoughtless faith,
adolescence, doubt . . . then skepticism, then disbelief, resting at last
in manhood's pondering repose of If. But once gone through, we trace
the round again: and are infants, boys, and men, and Ifs eternally."
—Herman Melville, *Moby Dick*

Doors

In sleep the ones departed
became doors but I must not have
remembered for waking I walked in
and out of the doors sometimes pausing touching
a door as if I'd left something I needed
or was waiting and all that time the door
only separated me from another *room*
that word so full of its own still
wind or sometimes like an ocean secretly
invisibly rocking its objects
back and forth back and forth but I got
older and the rooms grew smaller
and smaller and suddenly I was tall
as the hour and the daydream
terribly long and there were the toys
yesterday and tomorrow
I could finally pick up and hold.

One

Theory

A child's running hard toward the height of a man,
running, picking up shiny objects along the way,
and the man, having built a great tower, is gazing
down, squinting, trying to find the child. —To raise

memory to the vividness of the present. It was
a moment of hands, eyes, salt. Sheets, white, knew
flesh and let it sink. He remembers a blue shirt
slipping off a hanger. That was long ago, almost

a life. Now I'm learning to feel the invisible bones
of her face, dressing them with my own
dissolving touch. One theory of time's a moving knife's
edge, reflecting all, and all that it touches shines.

Voice, Distant, Still Assembling

Walking farther there, I am glad we
> age slowly, discovering now in memory
>> similar frontiers of a physical world, visiting
as though for the first time
>> ruins of a once great city, yet novel

>> in the crumbling light. We trip
and stumble, unaware, youthful in the obscurity
> of shadow, a kind of spring
in itself. *Itself*, where I touch places, gone, often
>> confused to find a new home
not torn and built of green, but of a crumbling

orange, and *there, there*, as though walking
>> through fire, taking pleasure in the fleeting
walls and lingering agoras, I glimpse
> ghost bodies and caress the flesh
>> boats of their past as I walk toward
> what could be mountains or oceans, till finally
I am swimming through the lit window of a name.

The Irises

The irises were so beautiful I had trouble
leaving. One day, one day it will be lonely
when people go. I wanted to linger a bit
longer among irises. Some white, some purple,
some pale blue. What can one say among
irises? One's speech grows dumb as they touch
the air. I wanted to linger a bit longer
among irises. The moment moves. Are you
ready? I think the body's a mansion
with two doors, one luminescent and open,
one dark and closed. I wanted to linger
a bit longer among irises. I felt something
opening into the room among our tangled
arms. One day, one day it will be lonely. Petals,
paper doors, walls, clouds. I wanted to,
you wanted to. That your desire may spill
into eternity, an impatience whose lingering is all.

Poem

Such a long way through darkness then a chance to sing.

Autumn seemed to mirror something as indiscernible as it was
green.

—Grass, straw, flame. The distance between each
is a sleep of seconds. What city would you
build?

And the air became rock, the earth
air, the fire
water, and the water a cloud we could feel
whose rain and spring sunlight

waited. And you could not breathe but were called. And you
waved and waved and waved
till the centuries of it
arrived.

Paradise

How all the thoughts, gestures
of a life are finally
swallowed in the gone
flesh. I remember thinking
this as a kid, staring
into a pond
at my face and clouds
but perhaps no one

really dies but
enters the Untime
where people move
just as we do
fearing a time when
they can no longer
be silent, but must shatter
the water's surface

we call a life. Paradise
becomes the in
between, the border
where a glance vanishes
on the taupe hide
of a deer
becoming shadowy
trees. We are

always passing one
another, pressing the invisible
coins of our eyes
into the felt but
unseen. "Don't worry,"
I want to tell
that child. "Your father
went to the Untime

where people speak
the language of
None, a humming
easily mastered that
sounds like the distant
ocean and feels
like stars across the back
of an October field."

The Nest

In the room lit by one candle in a white building,
you could hear the whining of jets and the shivering
roar of trains. We sat in a circle as the man
handed out slips of paper and asked us
to write down the hardest thing in each of our lives.
Then he asked us all to return at the same time, one
week later. We did and sat in the same places
as he picked up the pieces of paper and began to read:
"forgiving my brother who raped me when I was
ten"; "saying goodbye to my mother as she slowly
died"; "watching the hate in my son's eyes as he left
and never returned." When he finished reading, all
the pieces of paper became birds, that room a dark forest.
We returned each week to hear them screeching, singing,
screeching, as the sun rose and kindled the bright leaves.

Elegy (With Advertisement) Struggling to Find its Hero

It was a century in which we touched ourselves in mirrors
over and over. It was a decade of fast yet permanent
memories. The kaleidoscope of pain

some inflicted on others seemed inexhaustible
as the positions of *sex*, a term
whose meaning is as hybridized as the latest orchid. Terrorism

had reached a new peak, and we gradually
didn't care which airline we got on, as long as the pilot
was sober, and the stash of pretzels, beer, and soft drinks

remained intact. On TV, a teenage idol has just crawled, dripping wet,
from the top of a giant Pepsi can, or maybe I imagined it,
flicking through channels where the panoply

of *reality shows* has begun to exorcise
the very notion of reality, for both the scrutinized actor
and the debilitated viewer who becomes confused and often reaches

into the pastel screen for his glass, while down Broadway
sirens provide a kind of glamorous chorus
for this script of history where everything is so neatly measured

in miles, pounds, or megabits. How nice it would be
to drowse in the immeasurable. How nice
it would be to escape.

> *And there's a wobbly marble bench*
> *beneath an out-of-focus tree on the Web*
> *I like to occasion my body with.*

How brief we've become in our speed
I think. How fast the eternal.
How desperately

we need a clearing, a place
beyond, but not necessarily
of nature. *And the rain*

was so deep the entire forest smelled of stone, then the sun
broke, burying the long shadows
in gold. And the wounded

king woke in a book long since closed, and the princess
came to in a bed so large
she could never leave. How desperately

we need a new legend, one with a hero, tired
though he may be. One who has used
business to give up

business, one who has bought
with his heart what we
sold with ours.

When I Died,

I saw a man tearing down a blue house

but inside the blue house a green house

slowly appeared as the man motioned

toward me, suggesting I enter, opening

a white door where the man became

a woman in a yellow field with snow falling

upon so many people walking toward

a blue house, and they were telling each other

they had never seen anything so green,

not even the grass under the red sky of their names.

Psalm

And the tide came in and the tide went out. And when the sun set
over the burnt trees and toppled buildings, there was
a gilded loss.

And each of us had a little book, and we began
to gnaw on it till the words came
or we remained

dumb and silent. And each of us had a little stick
with which to walk, and we leaned
on them and looked over all

we had ruined. And each of us had a little bowl
and each began to pour its
contents into

another, and we did this over and over until all
the bowls had been poured and were
empty, then we

all smiled, holding nothing, and were happy.

Joy

A fresh slaughter of light on the water

and I was on my way home. Home's fresh slaughter

of hellos hung in the air and we were all smiles, smiles

slaughtered by laughter, laughter slaughtered by

food, talk, and family sleep slaughtered

by dreams, light, and the new day as we said our

goodbyes, looking, slaughtering the air with our hands.

Little Opus, Leaning, at That

In a large book made out of woods and sky, days
of my youth unfurl.

I tug each one like a kite, while some
tug back, or draw me away with their people, animals,
words. There's my father, smiling, walking

through a summer door, carrying evening in his lapels.
There's my dog Rocket chasing fireflies into the night.

And there's the word *mica* I discovered one tall hour
like a sheaf of translucent days I'm still peeling
the skin and light from. Soon

it will be autumn when every tree is a clock
and all the people wave their hands.

Crickets banjo in the tall grass
as night melts like chocolate
around them.

Landscape with Ball, Then Smeared with Shadow

Standing by home plate, he throws the white ball up
then hits it toward me in the field, all the Blue Ridge Mountains

beyond, and I'm running under it, trying
to judge the arc of its

fall and how, as he taught me, the wind
like time will carry an

event. *(We played*

on Sundays after church and, walking all the way
to that field, I'd pound my fist

into the cowhide palm and smell its sweat, like that of his Hat

beyond.) White dot against blue getting
larger, and I'm planting one foot and see

on that tree line (rain now on each black coat carrying
a rose) opened ground. "Keep your eye

on the ball." —Wind, white smack of the closet door
I open to a shirt (forty years) whose body's gone.

Call

Then through this lit sleep we call a life, I smell something enormous
blossoming,

        and the rain (its lengths) the inches and miles of it
saying *leap, shatter, give,* make
yourself whole till the end of each flower's a hand

that grows. Now I hear the sunshine of a little horn
        and I know a hero's
about to depart. He's picking a tulip he'll go
    to hell for, while birds cast silver nets

with their song. Thank God for the grass, its sex
   green & thick, upon which the hero will pull himself up
and say *sky,* while we stand dumb in our blue helmets and stare.

Two

Tall If

It had something to do with the flowers, their brief tents
and ballast of color, and with the pollen
spilled like gold sugar onto the lawn.

It had something to do with each of our
lives, when we stood between evening
and forever, and someone

spoke and the words made a kind of grass
all over the page. We
waited there, picnicking

in that brief summer. Yesterday I planted
the seeds, and today their fire
leafs, climbs. I will

water the fire till that fire greens
between red sky and blue
earth. Fool,

this is the way time
works. One minute the salt
becomes sugar, or the flesh you

held becomes distant as cloud, or slow
and perfect as stone. —Privileged
moments when the light

comes out of the air and stands unused
for a while. And so we walked
out of our minds

into the sky, ignorant of each gesture
calling us back, the glittering
armor on the ground.

American Urn

A wide prairie dotted with buffalo finding some mountains.

A machine on a long track moving west: People in feathered

costumes. —Flags, a slaughter. Below, a war with this flag

and another that, as you turn the bronze, becomes a modern

riot. Now a metropolis and airport, a radio tower,

then a dead tree that resembles a cross as the images become

more cluttered—an ad for soap that will make you younger,

a tiny action figure staring into the distance, and an enormous

shine from I can't tell what, but could be the evening

with all its bright tons settling down over wheated fields.

Aria (With a Hole in It)

*—Nellie Connally: 40th anniversary of the J.F.K.
assassination*

Now the last surviving occupant of the Lincoln convertible, now

      in a luxurious condo, towering above Houston, now

bringing out the hot-pink, Neiman-Marcus suit, cleaned, still

      in a plastic bag after 40 years, she begins retelling it all—

the motorcade sailing down Elm Street through the jubilant

      crowd. Now she stands by the window and begins

her aria. "Mister President," she says, "Mister President,

      you certainly can't say that Dallas doesn't love you." Then

the motorcade snaps, comes apart like something from

      the neck of History. And now, in a lower octave, "It was

a car full of yellow roses, red roses, and blood . . .

all over us." Now she's seated on the couch, looking down,

and the years go tumbling by as she holds that tremolo.

      And now in this one room she's fidgeting with her hands,

she keeps fidgeting with something invisible like she's trying to

      reassemble a newspaper read by too many people.

Sunday

Something happened, such that now our casual
lingering seems almost haunted. Do we seem
to wait more on Sundays? The scenery's much more
still, as if someone set glass weights of patience *here*.
How filled with earth that word, and so we walk, stare
at the inching leaves, read a book, or ignore those chores
on this first day of the week that feels more like the last,
perhaps because the past seems easier, as if the big, unread
newspaper could fill it, yet sparks of something lie
hidden, waiting to ignite into a blaze almost no one would
notice. Sunday has no verbs. Perhaps that's why I recall places,
people, or feel again a name separate from life, then fill
with the air of memory, a dumb balloon, one that sometimes
floats, one that I reach up toward and always almost grab, then
the stones turn into a kind of language. Perhaps I should call
home. I mean the one where now a few ghosts live, for there,
too, the world's a gilded stasis, while secretly the ambulance
of my unconcern's waiting like that cat wiping the robin's
blood from his mouth with one paw, half watching for tomorrow
to light upon a branch, feathers in the green fire of limbs
opening beyond, for freedom must always be far from death.

Weight of Light

The mirrors in dining and living room
seemed to catch us for
a while, just as those flashes from cameras

did. Distant, they now seem sugary
things we could pluck from a tree and eat, and we
do. —Look, children carry

little skulls of ice cream, licking them, as sunlight
licks the houses all the way down
the street. And over there

people stand in line, and what is being
paid out cannot be counted
or changed. Soon they

will hike to a lake, and wonder, and dip their hands
into a sheen there, then later in the story
rub it all across their

bodies. Somewhere
in the distance, someone's
holding the X-ray of all this up toward

sky, and while we
look down, that person continues
to look up, nodding slowly.

Yes

Sometimes in the middle of each April
when the dandelions stare
through our sleep, when the cellophane, torn,
glints in the teeth of grass, and the squirrel lobs its orange fire

limb to limb, I am content to gaze into the air engraved
with sparrows and rain, into the wonderfully out-of-focus
green in all its flux. Then the word *yes*
finds all its creeks and rivers, then our cries
are urgent and palpable as gravel thrown
into water. Surprised we
blink and are taken. Then I remember

that my question, having something to do with light, has come
a long way, and now I would like to tell you
something else in the language of petals, something about winter
and the stones placed upon so many dead.

Concrete

Sand, gravel, water, cement—an amalgam, as their lives
became an amalgam. The trees were making buds
and fuzzy leaves while he was pouring

into the forms. —Elk vanishing in the mountains, bison
on the plains. Inside the house, smell of baking bread.
Now adding a little water and troweling it smooth.

Now placing their daughter's handprint on it
between each of theirs. Brief smell of the ocean, history
breathing through an hour. A cloud covers

a house in shadow, and now it's raining, raining.
That it might never dry. He would like to finish
his painting: *Still Life with Cat and Caught*

Sparrow. She would like them to be
married. Catkins shiver in the late sun. Dalliance
of a young couple kissing. She says, "Sometimes there's crushed

shell in the lime." In the mountains a glacier's
melting. —Tide of shadow through the trees. *The feathers*
seem sharp like tin and are shining. —A thousand
ages like an evening gone. The sidewalk to their house is drying.

Now

Walking out of the cabin, leaving the grey picture
of them behind, he gazes up at stars. Yes
he'd once swirled, a wet thumb in her belly. The body,
its small unholy history, and the body, its anomaly
cast in stars: Braille to our intellect. *A cake once*
he'd baked her, the cake unlighting its candles as
she leans toward them in the grey photo. Her breath
aimed toward darkness, while now through the window
the fire aims toward him. The fire, compare it to
the folly of hands, but the flesh lit within, how
it gleams. He would like a word for it now, a sound
he would click on and save like that of the river's
slow hum that would continue to carry him through
the river of hands, legs, arms—this swimming
we do with the body, the body that must enter or be
entered by another. Again, looking up, he
thinks of those in the photograph, unfazed by the time
streaming behind them. *He poured flour and sugar into a bowl,*
flour speckled all over his black turtleneck. Next to his foot
the woodpile, and on the blade of the axe he can almost read
something, a shine like that on the back of his father's
watch, its small sweaty mirror he'd like to swim into. *A cake*
rising in the oven, a flower, warm, opening in the middle
of winter. "Happy birthday," he said. Times when the body aches
to sound in a word. The smell of butter and burnt sugar lingers.
How many eggs? Three. How many years? —All of them.

Heart

As he opened the sternum
I saw the heart
bubbling and red
in its cage
the working lips
of paradise
hidden in
that dark stadium
where the lion the bull
the sheep of our
desires our fears
wait over and over
it beat
like something both
epic and tired a
superman's shrunken
cape within which
another something
was wanting, waiting to
burst, spill, spell, body
over and beyond
its viscous tent.
Who now is fumbling
the reins, whipping the hide
taking me home?

The Field

I like the field best in winter when it's a giant bug

lying on its back, when its legs

are trees walking through sky. And I know

because they buried you in a field

the bug will right itself in a great spring

wind, dragging limbs through the earth, roots

through the clouds, and though you'll be

gone, I will have lost nothing

for that creature will carry the dead

like eggs to another earth

where they will swarm, and all our

remembering will be invisible tracings

in a familiar wind on a different sky.

Epic Detour

Forgive me, I was naive and easily led astray, always
    saying *yes* on the lost path, and *please*
while thieves picked my pockets clean.

To some I might have appeared—

A boy, blond in the twilight, carrying an atlas
    almost as big as himself, tilting it—north, west,
east, south—never quite locating paradise.

There was a shining city and behind that a shadowy
    forest where animals roved and our bodies
were taken. They sent me there to tell our stories

which were mocked, derided. I learned their language
    of razors and gears from which we made
a smaller city, an effigy in one of our fields. We

still give tours that lead up to it from our woods. You
    enter, opening a steel door and stare into the noise.

Résumé

Childhood games, first words, then sex & God, no
need to continue, but those first words
dug holes—Mother (milk, garden), Father (gasoline, bridge)—
growing deeper, then later the verbs
that shadow and leave
we call bodies till once in the ambulance
of my desire that love letter
became *Will*, the clouds
green, the land a motion beneath my feet
steep & purple.

Three

Gone

—for Willis Barnstone

When we arrived from that world of 30,000 sleeps, some
who had forgotten asked how it was,

and moved by their pleas I replied. There
we wore suits of flesh, and with these
thought we loved, sometimes
pairing off for a life.

There, some of us prayed, others made art, but most
bought and sold things over and over
as if they were building

something. And every day there was either a lottery,
or a sacrifice, gleaming red on
a hill while others watched
in joy or fear.

There was a place with wide, palm-lined avenues
and casinos on either side where people
bet on wheels, cards, dice, which made them feel
alive and what they thought was happy.

I said that in spring, marveling at the green earth
and wet air, we made excited sounds with our red tongues and
        polished language
like so many twittering birds, except that we
were unable to lift our bodies.

I said that we were a small, blue-green planet, a chrysalis
turning gray and brown, hung from a galaxy's
lit-arm, and that when you wake up

you would be here.

Passage

The dull gold light shone in the snow
as we walked into the cold barn.
How many of us came from sleep? How
many of us now believed only in invisible
things? We stood in line and walked
single file up toward a small fire
where he stood. One by one we opened
our wallets and paid him in straw.
We were buying days in autumn, summer,
spring. I bought a day in April when
the sun played like a horn all over the new
stubby green. We were so hungry for more
days. Why were we so patient? All shadow,
he took our money and never said a word.

Landscape Crossed with Sleep & Prayer

The stars are not real, not
the trees, the lake. How far it is
to another body. How fast the mind's
leap. Now I lay me down
to the dead. Their names are still windows
to a doorless place. I would only ask them
where, for what are places when we
sleep? Now I lay me down to be
the object of what will soon be lost.
To what or to whom should I pray?
That tomorrow you be exactly hungry
beside me. The stars and trees are not real. I swim
across the lake of your body. I drown. I wake.

The Mountain

Cruel fantasy I often think, climbing through shadow and trees, looking up
at rock, cloud, and snow. Yes, the snow here, there, in patches tells we're
getting closer, for our only window's the snow, its peak a light left on all

> day, a chalky skull beneath stars
> at night where we gaze,
> forgetting time. Some feel that the spatial
> does not exist here, that the mountain
> is time, and where it
> stops, the moment vanishes,
> for those who have tried to draw the mountain

have failed, for how can one draw time? —all snow burning the white paper
toward cloud? Is it then the mountain lounges back to encounter us in all our
graceless effort? Halfway up one sees smoke, intense heat, but no

> flames, though many have looked. Are
> we the fire, burning through the marching
> air, destroying what we
> search for, where young and old
> meet, desirous and forgetful at once
> in this great tent where we've
> slept and dreamed

our lives? Climbing up the steep face we pass streams, rivulets, and brooks,
where sometimes we pause, place our hands and drink, then describe the
place to others, calling this language. Once I saw some young people
dragging a word

> up. What was it? Sometimes I think our climbing
> is a question we can't quite
> phrase, though we've all dreamed
> its formulation, and though there are many stories
> of those who've reached the top, all details
> seem to vanish, for the white reaches
> of snow make us

forget, while sometimes our desire, like snow in water, seems to dissolve. Here, our hopes and despairs become confused like the seasons, for it's always spring or winter while we're climbing. Maybe everything's just too large, though once in dream

> I was a giant and moved
> the mountain with my finger, where many
> swarmed like ants on something sweet, transitory. Some
> say there's a poem about the mountain, a poem
> found in the snow. A woman quoted me
> these lines: "Where will you go
> once you reach the summit? Then what could you

possibly say in the language of snow?" Is the mountain a bell too close to hear, ringing of all things forgotten, all things left to discover? I will never forget the young man, saddened, coming down in spring. He claimed

> there was no snow, just
> ash, that a fire, invisible, was
> this mountain. Words turned to water
> in his mouth. I remember
> squinting through the impossible glare. His youth dissolved
> before my eyes, and on that morning
> he vanished.

Home

After your death I stopped on the hill and looked down at our house,

but as I approached it did not grow larger. Finally I bent down,

picked it up, and put it in my pocket. Now I can never

return, but sometimes I'll place that house by my window

and watch the tiny, shadowy figures move. If only I could make myself

small again, but the years. Sometimes I see clothes, bodiless, spill

through that house, a kind of light, then I wake, gripping the sheets.

In one dream I live in a vast country atop a pebble. When people

in this country die, they become larger, robbing more and more

space from the living, yet they continue to evolve, building smaller

houses, raising fewer children, writing smaller and smaller books,

until finally everyone thinks for a long time before uttering a word.

A Brief History of Eternity

They were sitting by a lake in the mountains, the light
swimming around their bodies beneath one
cloud and tree. One looking down from a distance
would have seen the forest and jeweled lake
as locket, the words they were speaking
as key. They were so close,
having come so far into the silence.
Their hopes and memories lay strewn about
like brightly disheveled clothes. The sun shone. She
had a small gold bird in her pocket
he'd given her long ago. They both wanted
so much for it to sing.

Icon

I'm holding the blue pencil
I bought from the armless, legless
man at the foot of the Academia
Bridge. I'm holding the blue
pencil, remembering how
he mouthed my lire
note, dropped it in a cup,
then rocking, rocking back
and forth, fell face first on
the blanket, picking up other notes,
coins he placed, moist
in my hand though I insisted
I wanted none. He kept
rocking, picking up, sometimes
dropping the coins. It was
December, a cool Sunday
morning but he was sweating,
bobbing, sometimes twirling
to pick the coins up
in the minutes or hours of
the exchange. My hesitation,
his eagerness and incredible will.
I remember at one moment
his chin on my open hand.

Stadium

—Stadium of sorrow where archeologists dig for a jet's brief fossil.

Stadium, a bit of immovable Latin fixed like a huge stone within our
more tensile English language; stadium, from the Greek *stadion*,
fixed measure of length, altered from *stadios*, standing. Stadium,
a track (for footraces or events) surrounded by tiers of seats for
spectators. Stadia, the plural, and also a method of surveying in
which distances and elevations are obtained through the use of
graduated stadia rods.

Stadium, an incantatory word, especially when repeated (due to
the fixed hum in the third syllable), akin to that of the Sanskrit *om*,
intoned as part of a mantra, or as a mystical utterance of assent
during meditation.

—Stadium, a place where people or distances are united or lost.

Stadium of sorrow: How dark into the far do the dead sail?

9/11/01

Hello

Hello, hello you say to the echoes now

and to the grapes hello.

Hello in sunlight as though you were looking

through your own lit flesh. Hello hello to the lengthening shadows

and to the snow now and to how

you fear. Hello hello

to those who rise in sleep now

and greet you now so

far from home.

$$\frac{54}{55}$$

Four

Blueprint for Civilization Sometimes Lost in Frivolous Detail

His archeological site's a junkyard where the lost sound of a car horn
becomes a city's screams of terror and joy.

* * *

The Abercrombie & Fitch ad shows the sweaty flanks and torsos
of boys moving toward a goal we could only guess
is youth multiplied by victory.

* * *

"And the Ancient of Days took his seat. His clothing was white as snow;
the hair of his head white like wool."   —Daniel 7: 9-10

* * *

The cartoon showed Road Runner, having overshot the cliff's
edge, gazing down into pure consciousness, then the mad
scramble back to this earth.

* * *

She said to me, "To be close to God you have to go through a series
          of events.
You don't hear of many people speaking in tongues while they're
doing the dishes."

* * *

The traffic leads toward bleachers surrounding a spectacle.
And if you were to uncode the tall glass and concrete, what would
remain? —A forest leading up to a desert that becomes sea
where an immense orange light shines.

Church Engine

The long wail of a red-faced infant become silence,

schooled laughter, adult speech, then come-cry

after he kisses his bride around which mourners later try

to gather the years, saying *she was so young*. Sometimes now,

half a century later, wheezing for breath, he remembers snow,

as spring rain then sunlight begin drenching the green.

What I Remember

What I remember most of death
was how we kept trying to build something. What
was it? What I remember most about death
were the extensive travels—the stairways
through levels and degrees of shade—when in fact
we went nowhere. What I remember most about death
was the continual desire to love in the gaining darkness,
which is like a train crossing a bridge of feathers.
What I remember most about death was how each day
spread a tablecloth of light over nothing, and how
we would eat there, gazing into the darkness, gorging
ourselves without hands.

Liminal, Bridal, Tremulous

1.

Even me out now toward those with nothing—
all the doorways become walls
mansioning

light. Annie said she could feel
her body die, then come
back to life

2.

with the chemo. —A suture, a rock,
a wedding vow. I take
this feather

spackled with blood and yolk
into a cave, then blow
till it becomes

3.

a fire. The day calves an inexhaustible glow, gold-
struck, that runs across
the field. We call

this morning and are glad.

Ars Poetica

The tree limb broke and the small branch in my hand
became pencil. I wrote and wrote and wrote.
There was light (shuddering through a green

canopy) and darkness. Children sang, lovers romped, while the old

smiled back over the fleeing, illumined
triangle of it (called house), remembering how the words were once
places, acts, and the names were bodies

moving, giving in the light
played all at once that broke on the white page
where a little music (birds glimpsed from a distance)

staggered up and, in the new glare, sang.

Soul?

Agency of what? —This trunk we call
body? And beyond the fence
of age, where do you
go? To what
can I compare thee? As water is like

nothing else. As ocean
is immense. The soul knows this, speaking the language
of give, and grows

fat, speaking with wide hands. I give you
my hat in the wind, my heart
invisibly

tall. What
else? By you
I have been glimpsed through. Are you
what I feel when someone's
staring? This ply

we can't explain on flesh's
nothing. Tacit
you are, as animals make a kind

of higher music without
sound. Once a fly
rode with me from Ohio to Nebraska, though
I was still companioned
when it'd

gone. Soul, what nebulous
ichor have you
if any?

Long Portrait

The snow coming through that X-ray is a mountain
no one can reach, but through a season's
melting becomes your bones.

Like it or not we belong to the dark.

Look, daffodils unfold beneath a jet's roar
while a red ball rolls across the lawn.

Remembering, I threw the spoon I fed you with into the ocean.

Love's the celebration, flesh the dangerous ice cream.

Twilight settles like the weightless talk of children.
—Stars, then a grave.

The Lastingness of Things Only Occurs in
a Brief Light

In our sleep the questions were giants. They lifted us up
in their arms, then whispered something we always forgot.

Time moves faster the farther we get from the center.
—How to find the swift stillness in each place.

Between *is* and *was* I found a slippery porch and receding
door. Tell your story in all its joy and sorrow. Use as few
words as possible, for adjectives would be useless to any god.

The imprint of two bodies in the spring grass,
then snow swirls along the bank and channels of ice.

The light we see never ends. It crashes to earth, caresses
and slaps us, then sails through our blood. Over the years

it makes a waterfall of each hand, raiment upon raiment.
Drowned, you will see that oblique flash again through darkness.

Searchlight

The church now seemed a hole in the sky

that day would swallow with sun, then evening
came. Sometimes I think it's the white paper shining through words,

but we kept walking, joying or grieving in it.

What we remember and what we fail to—that flash, glow, then nothing.

Look up, in all that shining an astronaut's on his knees
looking for something he lost there.

When I woke to the numbers—their order all dark there—I was afraid.

Wings of a plane cross the sun, tossing the brief skirt of something upon us.

We could hear the water, but we couldn't see it. We could see
the words, but we didn't understand, and we followed
him, or his ghost, but we didn't know
where or why.

Eurydice & Orpheus

Long her darkness there, his turning head
        a seed, his longing the imagined foliage not
come, his uncertainty the yellow
        leaves. "The *here* is her," he said, over and over

without turning round. *Wait* he kept
        thinking, and he waited in that waiting
and knew every time we speak we stun
        the word, so he hummed, but the humming

grew, each bee'd syllable toward
        a name, and as he turned
almost surprised to read its sign—*Eurydice*
        Eurydice—now the radio of his voice

dismantling sound. How terrible and free
        he stood, watching, no longer
waiting, then she picked her beauty up
        like a shovel and was gone.

Politics

Against the horizon those sheep resemble mountains. His

red tie a piece
of meat butchering his
shirt. Bored during the debate, the child

(vultures circling above)

paints the entire town blue, each of the people
white. He calls them the Clouds—

Mary, Bill, and Helen Cloud.

Fat, smoking, laughing men throw
dice. —Reversed stars. What if the sheep don't move? And there's

a giant walking so far ahead of our lives he appears small.

Panels

As

she looked at me, or through me, trying to photograph
the rain, and said the present doesn't really exist, the fetching
present, as the sky pushed open clouds, birthing rags
of light like snow, as she said this, her face a cameo of fire, the camera's
hinged greedy eye feeding on the bloated seconds as she
spoke filmy words, backing away, snapping shot after shot, I watched
the steps through trees the light makes, and then the darkness, the gradual
feathering shadows, a silence that seemed to want to fly.

A Gate

is always there, invisible to some, visible to others
perhaps passing, pausing to turn, to hold the light
Yes the sunlight breathing upon faces warm in the late
amber pulling *Yes* pulling the moment out oblong
swelling it all over the faces that in the swollen
light flower and open the new space out
with colors flushing warm you want to follow, touch,
hold with the light pulling the moment *Yes* long into sky
holding its shine, pulling it now *Yes* always *Yes* and never enough.

Ends

All that we did here—talking, reading, sleeping—
I thought was a building of sorts, but the doors grew tired
and flew away in search of another house.

—So many names whose bodies are gone. They are jars
we store in dark closets, but sometimes light
gets in and they shine.

Ocean—all day—doing its grand back and forth, and from the shore
fire watched, diminishing, then our breaths
applauded and were gone

as we began to rehearse the different versions. Each of us
dressed as a season, then waited to change
or be changed while the snow on that hill resembled an enormous
egg whose green wings were already ahead
of the melting story, the one that will never rise.

After

There, there are,
after you have forgotten
everything, babies, thousands

      of babies, each with its
      pink hand trying to lift
      a stone—there are so many stones

and there is no wind
but a lifetime of events begins
blowing, blowing past

      like knots in a kite's tail
      spaced at a great distance,
      and who is running,

breathlessly holding a tall
weight while leaning
over green fields?

$$\frac{72}{73}$$

photo by Nolan Rucker-Sauvage

Mark Irwin was born in Faribault, Minnesota, in 1953, and has lived throughout the United States and abroad in France and Italy. His poetry and essays have appeared widely in many literary magazines including *Antaeus, The American Poetry Review, The Atlantic, Georgia Review, The Kenyon Review, Paris Review, Poetry, The Nation, New England Review*, and the *New Republic*. He has taught at a number of universities and colleges including Case Western Reserve, the University of Iowa, Ohio University, the University of Denver, the University of Colorado/Boulder, the University of Nevada, and Colorado College. The author of five previous collections of poetry, *The Halo of Desire* (1987), *Against the Meanwhile*, Wesleyan University Press (1989), *Quick, Now, Always*, BOA (1996), *White City*, BOA (2000), and *Bright Hunger*, BOA (2004), he has also translated two volumes of poetry, one from the French and one from the Romanian. Recognition for his work includes The Nation/Discovery Award, four Pushcart Prizes, National Endowment for the Arts and Ohio Art Council Fellowships, two Colorado Council for the Arts Fellowships, two Colorado Book Awards, the James Wright Poetry Award, and fellowships from the Fulbright, Lilly, and Wurlitzer Foundations. He lives in Colorado, and Los Angeles, where he currently teaches in the Graduate Creative Writing Program at the University of Southern California.

Acknowledgements

I would like to thank the editors of the following magazines where many of these poems first appeared.

AGNI Review: "Blueprint for Civilization Sometimes Lost in Frivolous Detail"

American Poetry Review: Panels: "As," "A Gate," and "The Nest," "Theory"

American Letters & Commentary: "Candidate," "Joy," "Long Portrait"

American Literary Review: "Ave Maria," "Now," "Passage"

Antioch Review: "Aria (with a Hole in It)"

Chelsea: "A Brief History of Eternity"

Colorado Review: "After," "Ars Poetica," "Doors," "Ends," "Searchlight"

Denver Quarterly: "Ends," "Church Engine"

88: "Heart"

FIELD: "American Urn," "Field," "What I Remember"

GULF COAST: "Résumé"

Georgia Review: "Icon," "Paradise"

Hotel Amerika: "Call," "Epic Detour," "Little Opus, Leaning, at That," "When I Died"

Hunger Mountain: "Tall If"

International Poetry Review: "Sunday"

Kenyon Review: "Elegy (With Advertisement) Struggling to Find its Hero"

Marginalia: "The Lastingness of Things Occurs in a Brief Light" "Weight of Light"

New Letters: "Gone"

POOL: "April in a Pail"

The New Republic: "The Irises"

TriQuarterly: "Eurydice & Orpheus," "Hello," "Poem," "Voice, Distant, Still Assembling," "Concrete," "Home," "Yes," "Psalm"

"When I Died" was reprinted as a Pushcart Prize Selection, volume XXVIII, 2004.

"Elegy (with Advertisement) Struggling to Find Its Hero" was reprinted as a Pushcart Prize Selection, volume XXX, 2006.

"The Irisies" was reprinted in *Western Wind*, 5th edition, McGraw Hill, 2005.

"Ends" was featured, and reprinted electronically on *Poetry Daily*: 1.25.06.

"Stadium" appeared in *9.11. 2001: American Writers Respond*, ed. William Heyen.

New Issues Poetry

Vito Aiuto, *Self-Portrait as Jerry Quarry*
James Armstrong, *Monument in a Summer Hat*
Claire Bateman, *Clumsy, Leap*
Sandra Beasley, *Theories of Falling*
Kevin Boyle, *A Home for Wayward Girls*
Jason Bredle, *Standing in Line for the Beast*
Jericho Brown, *Please*
Michael Burkard, *Pennsylvania Collection Agency*
Christopher Bursk, *Ovid at Fifteen*
Anthony Butts, *Fifth Season; Little Low Heaven*
Kevin Cantwell, *Something Black in the Green Part of Your Eye*
Gladys Cardiff, *A Bare Unpainted Table*
Kevin Clark, *In the Evening of No Warning*
Cynie Cory, *American Girl*
Peter Covino, *Cut Off the Ears of Winter*
James D'Agostino, *Nude with Anything*
Jim Daniels, *Night with Drive-By Shooting Stars*
Joseph Featherstone, *Brace's Cove*
Lisa Fishman, *The Deep Heart's Core Is a Suitcase*
Noah Eli Gordon, *A Fiddle Pulled from the Throat of a Sparrow*
Robert Grunst, *The Smallest Bird in North America*
Paul Guest, *The Resurrection of the Body and the Ruin
        of the World*
Robert Haight, *Emergences and Spinner Falls*
Mark Halperin, *Time as Distance*
Myronn Hardy, *Approaching the Center; The Headless Saints*
Brian Henry, *Graft*
Edward Haworth Hoeppner, *Rain Through High Windows*
Cynthia Hogue, *Flux*
Joan Houlihan, *The Mending Worm*
Christine Hume, *Alaskaphrenia*
Mark Irwin, *Tall If*
Josie Kearns, *New Numbers*
David Keplinger, *The Clearing; The Prayers of Others*
Maurice Kilwein Guevara, *Autobiography of So-and-So:
        Poems in Prose*
Ruth Ellen Kocher, *When the Moon Knows You're Wandering;
        One Girl Babylon*

Gerry LaFemina, *The Window Facing Winter*
Steve Langan, *Freezing*
Lance Larsen, *Erasable Walls*
David Dodd Lee, *Abrupt Rural; Downsides of Fish Culture*
M.L. Liebler, *The Moon a Box*
Alexander Long, *Vigil*
Deanne Lundin, *The Ginseng Hunter's Notebook*
Barbara Maloutas, *In a Combination of Practices*
Joy Manesiotis, *They Sing to Her Bones*
Sarah Mangold, *Household Mechanics*
Gail Martin, *The Hourglass Heart*
David Marlatt, *A Hog Slaughtering Woman*
Louise Mathias, *Lark Apprentice*
Gretchen Mattox, *Buddha Box, Goodnight Architecture*
Carrie McGath, *Small Murders*
Paula McLain, *Less of Her; Stumble, Gorgeous*
Lydia Melvin, *South of Here*
Sarah Messer, *Bandit Letters*
Wayne Miller, *Only the Senses Sleep*
Malena Mörling, *Ocean Avenue*
Julie Moulds, *The Woman with a Cubed Head*
Carsten René Nielsen, *The World Cut Out with Crooked Scissors*
Marsha de la O, *Black Hope*
C. Mikal Oness, *Water Becomes Bone*
Bradley Paul, *The Obvious*
Jennifer Perrine, *The Body Is No Machine*
Katie Peterson, *This One Tree*
Jon Pineda, *The Translator's Diary*
Elizabeth Powell, *The Republic of Self*
Margaret Rabb, *Granite Dives*
Rebecca Reynolds, *Daughter of the Hangnail;*
        The Bovine Two-Step
Martha Rhodes, *Perfect Disappearance*
Beth Roberts, *Brief Moral History in Blue*
John Rybicki, *Traveling at High Speeds* (expanded second edition)
Mary Ann Samyn, *Inside the Yellow Dress; Purr*
Ever Saskya, *The Porch is a Journey Different From the House*
Mark Scott, *Tactile Values*
Hugh Seidman, *Somebody Stand Up and Sing*
Heather Sellers, *The Boys I Borrow*
Martha Serpas, *Côte Blanche*
Diane Seuss-Brakeman, *It Blows You Hollow*
Elaine Sexton, *Sleuth; Causeway*
Marc Sheehan, *Greatest Hits*

Heidi Lynn Staples, *Guess Can Gallop*
Phillip Sterling, *Mutual Shores*
Angela Sorby, *Distance Learning*
Matthew Thorburn, *Subject to Change*
Russell Thorburn, *Approximate Desire*
Rodney Torreson, *A Breathable Light*
Lee Upton, *Undid in the Land of Undone*
Robert VanderMolen, *Breath*
Martin Walls, *Small Human Detail in Care of National Trust*
Patricia Jabbeh Wesley, *Before the Palm Could Bloom:*
       Poems of Africa